Let There Be Lights!

Let There Be Lights!
A Beginner's Guide to Outdoor Christmas Decorating

Christopher M. Donnells

iUniverse, Inc.
New York Bloomington Shanghai

Let There Be Lights!
A Beginner's Guide to Outdoor Christmas Decorating

Copyright © 2008 by Christopher M. Donnells

All rights reserved. No part of this book may be used or reproduced by any means, graphic, electronic, or mechanical, including photocopying, recording, taping or by any information storage retrieval system without the written permission of the publisher except in the case of brief quotations embodied in critical articles and reviews.

iUniverse books may be ordered through booksellers or by contacting:

iUniverse
1663 Liberty Drive
Bloomington, IN 47403
www.iuniverse.com
1-800-Authors (1-800-288-4677)

Because of the dynamic nature of the Internet, any Web addresses or links contained in this book may have changed since publication and may no longer be valid.

The views expressed in this work are solely those of the author and do not necessarily reflect the views of the publisher, and the publisher hereby disclaims any responsibility for them.

ISBN: 978-0-595-52106-7 (pbk)
ISBN: 978-0-595-62170-5 (ebk)

Printed in the United States of America

This book is dedicated to:

To my loving wife Ann I thank you for walking into my life on that cool summer night. You are the most special person in my life … my best friend. Your words of encouragement, as well as your love and support, make the most seemingly impossible dreams possible. I love you honey!

To my Dad, Thanks for your love, encouragement and support through the years. Even though I'm taller than you, I will always look up to you.

Without a Mom like mine, I truly don't believe that Christmas would be as special and meaningful as it is today. Mom, thanks for all that you did during my childhood to make those memories last until today and well into the future.

Contents

Prologue 1

Chapter 1   Safety First! 3

Chapter 2   Lights, Lights and More Lights 9

Chapter 3   Just Hangin' In There … Clips and More . 18

Chapter 4   Building Your Display 24

Chapter 5   Snakes in the Grass 58

Chapter 6   Watts Up With You? 62

Chapter 7   Protect Yourself! 67

Chapter 8   Tear Down and Storage 70

Chapter 9   Good Lights Gone Bad 73

Chapter 10 Get Known! Websites and Fundraising 76

Afterthought 81

Christmas Links Mentioned 83

Acknowledgements

Dad, thank you for supplying me with the detailed illustrations found within this book.

Ray, thank you for tirelessly adding circuit after circuit year after year.

Andy, I trust you as an electrician and value you as a friend.

Prologue

So, you want to start decorating your home for Christmas? Congratulations! This is a great hobby; one that everyone can enjoy, but beware it can put a pretty big dent in your pocketbook. Trust me. But that discussion is for another chapter.

Before I get started, I wanted to preface this book with a remark. Merry Christmas! We tend not to say that to each other anymore. We have all become so politically correct in saying, "Happy Holidays" that we are slowly forgetting about Christmas and the true meaning of the word. If you do not like me saying, "Merry Christmas" or using the word Christmas, that's too bad. Enjoy the book anyways! With that out of the way, I'd like to continue.

I started decorating our house the year after my wife Ann and I got married. Nothing too fancy, just about 1,500 lights outlining our house. Not that much in standards of exterior illumination, but nonetheless, it brightened up everyone's Christmas spirit. After the Christmas season was over and the lights were put away, everyone kept asking, "How many lights are you adding to your display next year?" Unfortunately, they seem to ask that every year. Well, you can't let your fans down. Can you? In 2007, we had 30,000 lights; of course, that will increase next year.

You may be thinking, "Boy, that seems like a lot of work for a month's enjoyment," but it is definitely worth it. The time and effort put into your display shows. Go around your neighborhood and you can tell the difference between the houses that didn't take a lot of time planning out their decorations and the ones who did … no matter how many lights they have on their homes.

This book is simple. It will start from the very basics such as the different types of lights on the market to designing and building your own display and everything in between. Everything contained within has been learned mostly from trial and error. There is no right or wrong way to decorate your home. Think of your house as a blank canvas. You're the painter. Your palette: Christmas lights. What you'll find yourself saying after each year is, "I can see some lights there," or "Maybe I can change that around over there." I can't tell you how many times, in the middle of December no less, that I've been laying in bed thinking about the next year's display. That's the fun part … designing it. I hope that you will gain some great ideas for your display from this book and have a good time decorating. Remember, this is a hobby, not a chore.

With that said, let's get started on our journey through the never-ending, burning a hole in your pocket hobby of Christmas decorating.

I wish you the very best in building your display! Have fun and enjoy!

Merry Christmas!

Chris

Chapter 1
Safety First!

Before we get started discussing lights, I want to preface this entire conversation by saying that I am not an electrician. I don't even play one on T.V. Electricity should be taken seriously as you are dealing with household current which is enough to kill you if you are not cautious. Since most of our work will be performed outside in the elements, you have to be even more careful. That is why I wanted to dedicate this chapter to understanding a few basics before delving into the types of lights on the market.

Remember always hire a professional electrician to do your electrical work.

Be safe. Be happy. Be alive.

Outdoor Use Only

Before continuing on, I want to touch on the importance of the meaning of *Outdoor Use Only or For Indoor/Outdoor Use*. For the most part, the lights that you purchase will, in most cases, be used for either indoor or outdoor use. It has been my experience that on some of the less expensive sets may be rated for indoor use only. Make sure that you check the label and it says for *Indoor/Outdoor Use*. Don't buy lights or decorations that say Indoor Use Only and use them outside. By doing so, you may cause a fire or be subject to an electric shock. On occasion, and this holds especially true for extension cords, it will be difficult to locate the verbiage. If the package isn't labeled clearly, look on the tag attached to the string of lights or the extension cord. It will refer to whether or not the product can be used outside.

Extension Cords

Extension cords can be pretty tricky and confusing. Walking into any home store, you will find lots of extension cords. During Christmas, you'll find green extension cords as well as the more popular, bright orange. Just because they're orange or green does not mean that they are approved for outdoor use. You must read the packaging or sticker. I was in a store and saw a bargain for extension cords … 9 feet long, orange color, only $2.99. When you have a bunch of lights, this really is a bargain. As I read the packaging more clearly, there were no noticeable markings. Once I read the sticker on the cord itself, it said, *"For Indoor Use Only."*

Besides making sure that you are using the proper extension cord, another consideration is the gauge of the extension cord. The gauge of an extension cord refers to the thickness of the wire and how much current that the cord can carry. Although miniature lights do not use a lot of power, if you have a big display, it is possible that you could overload the maximum amperage of the extension cord.

All extension cords will be marked with a gauge. The higher the gauge the smaller the wire and the less current the cord can handle. For example, a string of 100 miniature lights is approximately a 22 gauge wire and does not carry much amperage whereas a 50 foot 16 gauge extension cord though, can handle approximately 13 amps. Even though miniature lights don't use much power, when you start adding set after set to an extension cord, it can add up.

Another interesting point to take into consideration is the length of the extension cord. The longer the cord the less current it can handle. If we took the same 50 foot, 16 gauge extension cord which handles about 13 amps and made it a 100 foot cord, it would handle approximately 10 amps. My recommendation is only use a cord that suits the job (i.e. if you need to go 25 feet don't use a 100 foot cord). Also, it will save you money ... a 100 foot 16 gauge cord costs twice as much.

But, what if you're at a tag sale, not a home store? You want to know what the gauge is but there is no sleeve on the cord. If you look very closely at the cord, the manufacturer will imprint the gauge and wattage on the rubber housing. The tag attached to the cord should also have that information but over time, those tags do get worn out or torn off.

Tip: During the Christmas season most home stores bring in green outdoor extension cords and sell them with the Christmas merchandise. These extension cords are usually 10 to 25 feet long and will run approximately $10 to $15 per extension cord. If you don't mind orange extension cords, you can usually buy them up to 50 feet for about $5.00 in the electrical aisle. This will save you a lot of money as you're going to need quite a few.

Ground Fault Circuit Interrupter (GFCI)

I think most of us have either heard of Ground Fault Circuit Interrupters (GFI's) or have them installed in our home. Even though it is a safety device, this type of outlet is also a pain to us that use them at Christmastime. You probably have one near your sink in the kitchen or bathroom. The GFI is designed to protect us from being electrocuted. It does this by having a trip sensor, that when triggered, turns off the power to the outlet. For example, if you were using a hair dryer while standing over a sink full of water (which isn't a good idea to begin with), and you dropped the hair dryer into the sink, you run a very high risk of being electrocuted. If the hair dryer was plugged into a GFI, the circuit would have tripped and the power from the outlet would be shut off. The GFI comes equipped with test buttons to make sure that the outlet is functioning properly. It is a good idea to test your outlets monthly to make sure they are in good working order. If they are not, hire a professional electrician to come and diagnose the problem.

If you do not have any GFI's installed on the exterior of your home, mark this as the first thing you should do when preparing your Christmas display. Survey the outside of your home. Make a crude drawing of your home taking into consideration how many lights you're going to have and where they'll be placed. Next, take note of spots around your home that will make it easy for you to get power to your display. You wouldn't want to have an outlet in the backyard for a display in the front yard. This extra time to survey your house will also make it much easier for the electrician when they come out to install your outlets.

Finally, when you do have the electrician come out, make sure that he or she places each outlet on a "dedicated circuit." By having dedicated circuits for your lights, you know for certain that nothing else is running off the circuit draining power for the display. I have a friend that overloaded his circuit and every time he turned on the VCR, the lights went off.

GFI's can be quite a pain to deal with if you live in an area that gets snow or rain. As they are designed to trip when detecting water, they have a tendency to set themselves off if exposed to a lot of rain or snow. One way of not having the GFI trip is to keep your connections elevated off the ground. This not only will keep the display lit while it's wet outside, but is also a safety precaution in case the outlet decides to stop working. I recommend placing stakes into the ground and zip tie the electrical connection to the stake.

This will keep the connections elevated off the ground and out of potential soggy spots during rain or snow storms. To serve as a barrier between the wet weather and the connections, place a plastic freezer bag over the connections. This will keep wet weather out but still let the connections breathe. I have heard of people wrapping the connections with plastic wrap and duct tape. While an ingenious idea, it does have a flaw. If condensation does get in, and it will, it will stay in. There is nowhere for it to go, therefore, your GFI will continue to trip.

Later we will discuss the basics of load handling capabilities of circuits and the amount of lights a circuit can handle. But for now, let's get to the fun part. Lights!

Chapter 2
Lights, Lights and More Lights

There are as many lights on the market as there are Irish in pubs on St. Patrick's Day. The choices can be overwhelming, especially if you search the internet for Christmas lights. You'll be there for days.

What we're going to do is discuss the different types of lights that are on the market today, their uses, good and bad points and what to look for when buying lights (remember cheap means just that … cheap).

The types of lights we will be discussing are:
- Miniature Lights
- Icicle Lights
- Net Lights
- C-7 Lights
- C-9 Lights
- Rope Lights
- LED Lights

Miniature Lights

These are by far one of the most popular kinds of Christmas lights you will find on the market. As a matter of fact, you probably have some sitting in your attic or garage right now. Miniature lights are distinguished by their very small lights (hence the name miniature lights) and come in a variety of colors such as purple and orange for Halloween as well as multi-colored sets, solid colors and clear sets for Christmas. They are typically found in strings (meaning a line of lights) with as little as 35 bulbs to as many as 300 bulbs per string. Miniature string light sets are great for decorating just about anything. I like to think of them as the "general" or "all-purpose" type of light set. Most of your yard displays such as wire frame reindeer and most yard décor use miniature lights. Miniature lights come with replacement bulbs as well as bulbs that will make them flash. The replacement bulbs come in different voltages. Some sets take 2.5 volt bulbs while others take 3.5 volt bulbs. If you are buying aftermarket replacement bulbs, make sure you buy the right voltage or your set will not work properly. Flasher bulbs, on the other hand, are very distinguishable by their red tip and will make the light set flash on and off at a random rate. Both replacement "steady on" and flasher bulbs are inexpensive and can be bought in bulk.

Another consideration when purchasing miniature lights is the spacing between the bulbs. Miniature light strings are made with bulbs spaced between 2 ½ inches to 6 inches apart. We will talk more about why this is important in another chapter.

> ***Tip: If you have a string die on you and you cannot repair it, save the bulbs! I do this with many of my strings as I don't want to throw money away. You can always use the bulbs in another set when one goes out.***

Commercial versus Consumer Lights

There are different versions of miniature lights in the marketplace, including commercial and residential light strings. Commercial sets allow you to connect up to 6 sets of lights together. Residential sets, on the other hand, allow you to only connect 3 sets together. The reason why commercial sets can handle more is because their fuses can handle more voltage. If you tried to connect six residential sets, the fuses would blow. Of course, what do you think the price is for commercial? Double. Unless you are planning to own your own decorating business, or you're covering the Pyramids of Giza, you don't need to spend the extra money on the commercial sets. Residential sets are just fine.

Icicle Lights

You may have seen these types either on someone's home or in the stores. These lights are made to be a hung off of a gutter or overhang to imitate icicles that form in those places. Most icicle lights have clear bulbs, but you can find them in a variety of colors such as multi-colored and solid colors. My favorite color of icicle lights is blue. Blue offers a softer tone and adds a little more depth to the display than using all clear lights. One of the most discouraging parts of icicle lights is taking them out of the packaging. As these lights have different lengths of strands on the string to simulate icicles, it takes a little patience to straighten them. Over the course of a season, they will eventually loosen and will not require any additional straightening.

Net Lights

These are great for decorating bushes around your property. Net lights, when laid out, resemble a fisherman's net and have approximately 150 lights per set. The net typically covers area of about 8 square feet and two sets are good enough for the average sized bush. Also, the bulbs on the net lights are evenly spaced across the set so when placed on a bush, it gives a very uniform appearance. If you were to put strings around the bush, you may not get the type of uniformity that net lights offer.

C7 and C9 Light Sets

C7 and C9 light sets are very distinguishable from miniature lights due to the large size of bulbs each set uses. You probably have C7 lights in your house if you have night lights. C7's are typically thought of as a traditional Christmas light. They come 25 to a string and each bulb is two inches long. Bases of C7 bulbs are very small and narrow. In the industry, they are called candelabra bases. You can buy replacement bulbs for C7's but you don't have to worry about voltage with these bulbs as they are all the same wattage. These lights are typically used to outline gutters, roof lines and windows. Use them sparingly, use too many of them and you'll be seen by the International Space Station.

Just as with miniature lights, C7's also come in many different colors and nowadays, if one goes out, the rest remain lit. I remember as a small boy my father would have lots of these C7 lights on the tree. Back then if one bulb went out they all went out. Guess whose job it was to find the bad bulb? Yeah, you guessed it ... me!

C9 sets are the biggest Christmas light you will find. They are about 3 inches tall and have a bigger base (intermediate base) than the C7's and come in sets of 25. While I'm sure your energy company would thank you for using them as they draw a lot of power, their best application is on large scale projects. Businesses use them to outline the fascia of the building for the holidays. From far away they look amazing but if used on a small house, they look out of place. Live by this rule of thumb: if you don't have more than two stories, don't use C9's as they will overpower your display. C7's would be the biggest bulb I would use on a suburban display for aesthetic purposes.

As an aside, I did try C9's on my Christmas tree in my home one year. I would never recommend this to anyone. As I had over 100 C9 lights on the tree, you can imagine how warm it was in the living room. I don't think the heat ever kicked on that year, not to mention that I pretty much dried out the tree. What I'm trying to say here is, what I did is pretty much considered a fire hazard so don't imitate me!

Tip: With respect to the number of lights per string, only connect "like" strings to "like" strings (net to net, miniature to miniature, or C7 to C7) and only connect the maximum of 3 same sets together at once (Rule of 3's) unless the box tells you otherwise.

Rope Lights

Rope lights are very easy to identify due to the nature of the light. The lights in a rope light are very small and are surrounded by a protective plastic sheath hence the reason why they are called rope lights. You will find some wire displays have rope lights instead of miniature lights. One of the good things about rope lights is that you can make your own designs with the lights. With a few tools and special connections, you could make all kinds of signs and figures since these lights are meant to bend and twist. I tend not to use them because they are not as aesthetically pleasing as miniature lights. Also, the rope lights tend to draw more power needs more than a regular string of miniature lights.

For lights that will last you close to a lifetime and not put a strain on the local power grid, nothing could be better than Light Emitting Diodes or LED Lights.

LED Lights

Light Emitting Diodes or more commonly known as LED's, is the new wave of the future in Christmas decorating. The reason is that they draw very little power and last a long time. A typical set of incandescent lights will last you, if you're lucky, 2 to 3 seasons while a set of LED's have a life span of approximately 200,000 hours! For those of you who are bad in math, that's approximately 23 years. So, even though they cost a lot more, you'll end up saving big in the long run.

Currently, manufacturers make many different styles of LED's such as M5, C6, C7, and C9.

M5 lights are similar to regular miniature lights and come in 25 and 50 light string sets.

C7 and C9 resemble their brother and sister sets of the incandescent type just in an LED setting.

The C6 is another type of LED that is shaped more like a pinecone or strawberry making it narrower than C7s and C9s.

The biggest downside to making a display solely out of LED lights is the cost. Each string of lights (assuming a 50 light string) can cost upwards of $15.00 per string. When looking at how much miniature incandescent lights cost after Christmas ($0.50 to 1.00 per string), the LED can put a big dent in one's pocketbook.

As you can see, there are many choices for Christmas lights on the market. One can really get confused deciding what lights to buy. That is why I recommend having a game plan. The legendary Vince Lombardi would never march onto the field and say, "Okay guys, go win the game," without a game plan. The same thing goes for choosing the right type of light for your application. Have a game plan in mind as to what kind of lights you want in your display, how many lights you want, and how much you want to spend.

Power Consumption

Later on in the book, we will be discussing the power that different light sets will draw. Just as a reference guide, I've put them in order from the set that draws the least amount of power to the set that draws the most:

- LED
- Miniature Lights (including icicle and net lights)
- Rope Lights
- C7
- C9

Finding Cheap Lights

One thing I get asked a lot is where I find low cost Christmas lights. Just as some people sleep outside in the cold the day after Thanksgiving for the next best electronic device, I show up at the local home stores for the after Christmas sales when they open. You can save upwards of 75% off the cost of all Christmas decorations after Christmas, but don't wait too long, or you won't get what you want. If the lights go on sale for a dollar a string before Christmas and you know you need a set amount, then buy them at a dollar a string. That's better than the $5 to $6 you'll pay in the off season. You'd be amazed at what you can find. You can spend an entire morning going from home shop to home shop finding big discounts.

Now that we have gone through the different types of lights available, what do we do with them when we want to hang them? Of course, you could always staple them to your roof but that probably isn't the smartest idea in the world. Duct tape? Well, you might have found the 1,001st use for it but they probably won't stay up too long. Glue? Well, at least you'd never have to worry about taking them down!

Next up we're going to discuss the different clips available on the marketplace and how to use them for different applications.

> *Tip: Track the sales of Christmas lights via the internet. Home stores are known for putting lights on sale prior to the day after Christmas.*

Chapter 3
Just Hangin' In There ... Clips and More

It's not that hard to decorate shrubs or trees. But what happens when you want to decorate your chimney, roof and siding? Duct tape, staples, tacks and glue can work for some applications but for Christmas lights, I don't think so. Just as a carpenter has specific tools that he/she uses to complete a job, so do us for Christmas lights. What tool you use, or in this case clips, will depend on where you will be hanging lights. There are many clips in the marketplace and we will touch on the uses of each of the more popular ones. First and foremost, the multi-clip.

Multi/All-in-One Clips

As the name implies, these clips are great for multiple uses and for all kinds of lights. They handle miniature lights, LED's, C7's and even C9's. This clip is by far the most used clip in any display. Not only can you use any type of light string with these clips, they are also great for gutters and shingles as well.

During the Christmas season you can find these multi-clips in the home stores for about $5.00 a box. After Christmas, they're about 50 cents a box! So try and buy them after the holidays!

One of the great uses is as a shingle clip. Have you ever seen homes that outline their roof or each row of shingles with lights and wonder how do they do that? Shingle clips are the answer. They are relatively easy to use and do little harm to your roof. All you do is slip each clip under the shingle and the weight of the shingle will keep it in place. String the lights through the clip and voila! You're on your way to having a roof that can be seen by space! You may wonder if they will hold up during a wind storm and I can say from experience, "Yes!" We've had some wind gusts up to 50 mph during the winter season and the lights have remained on the roof with no problems. After the season is over grab one end of the light string and pull. The lights will slide off the roof and you can roll them up for next year.

> *Tip: Make sure that the lights are taught as they will tend to give a little with the changes in temperature. Also, space each clip about 1 to 2 feet apart in order to keep the lights from sagging too much.*

Another good use for multi-clips is using them to outline your gutters with icicle lights. Depending on what kind of gutter you have, you may have to jockey them into position, but they should fit. After the clips are in place, string the lights through each clip and you're done. Some gutter designs aren't very clip friendly. But, have no fear; they do make adhesive clips that work very well.

Adhesive Clips

Adhesive clips are relatively small (about a ½ inch in width and height) and are made out of clear plastic. The clips come with double-sided tape that is the same size as the back of the clip so you don't have to worry about cutting the tape to size. Before applying the adhesive clip, wipe down the spot where the adhesive clip will be attached with a little rubbing alcohol. After the spot is dry, attach the double-sided tape to the clip and stick it to the gutter. These should hold up just fine during the winter months if applied correctly. When you remove your lights at the end of the season, don't pull the lights … take them down gently so as to not remove the clip.

> *Tip: When applying the adhesive clips, try to do them during a warmer month such as late September or early October. I've had problems with the adhesive pads sticking when applied in cold weather.*

Siding Clips

For the 2007 Christmas season I decided to hang lights off the siding of my house. The dilemma I faced was how to hang Christmas lights off aluminum siding. Well, low and behold, I was able to locate siding clips. These clips are very easy to use and the best part is that you can leave them up all year long. You can buy them from any online store that sells Christmas lights (see appendix for web address of retailer) and usually come about 25 to a package for about $2.50. The clips look like the letter J and have a lip at the very top. To use the clip, you slide it under the siding and the lip will keep the clip in place. Space each clip one to two feet apart. Depending on the size of your home, you may need quite a few clips. After all your clips are up, string the lights so they lie on top of the clips. Pull the lights a little taut to take up some of the slack. The lights, just as with the roof, will tend to droop a little due to changes in the weather.

Quick Clips

Quick clips are best used in situations where you don't mind driving a small nail through a fence or railing as these clips are attached by small brad nails. Put the quick clip against the fence or railing and drive the brad through the clip into the fence. Space each clip about one foot apart and start hanging your lights. These clips can also be left up all year long which will save you time and money from one season to the next.

> ***Tip: Put the clips up first and then put up the lights. Don't slip the clips over the wire first and nail as you***

run the risk of either stripping the wire or breaking a bulb.

Brick Clips

You may be thinking, I want to light up the exterior of my home but my house is made out of brick. What am I to do? Again, the smart people in the Christmas decorating business have thought of everything. You can find a clip for your brick building as well. While they are a little more expensive than siding clips (close to $6.00 for a set of two) you don't need as many. The one thing you will need to do is measure your brick. Brick clips come in different sizes depending on the size of your brick. To attach them, place them over the face of the brick so that they slip over the top and the bottom of the brick. There is a hook on the front that will enable you to string the lights to them. Unlike the siding clips which are barely noticeable, you probably want to remove the brick clips at the end of the season as they are a little unsightly.

Suction Cups

Suction cups? Who would have thought a suction cup would be used in Christmas decorating. I use them quite frequently for trimming the windows. They come in all different sizes and have metal hooks attached to them. They are very handy for hanging garland, wreaths or even lights around a window. You may have problems with them falling off your windows if you buy real cheap suction cups. To ensure that they will maintain a solid grasp on the surface, wet the back of the suction cup before applying.

While there are many other clips we could discuss, the ones that we reviewed are frequently used in residential displays. About 90% of the time you'll find yourself using the multi/all-in-one clip, but it's nice to know that you have options if you want to take your display to the next level.

Chapter 4
Building Your Display

People ask me all the time, "How long does it take you to build the display?" or "When do you start building your display?" The answer? Pretty much after the display is down I start working on next year's display. Except for a few months out of the year (we all need a break); I'm working on the display year round in one way or another. Once you get bitten by the Christmas bug, you'll understand.

Painting Your Canvas

Before artists begin painting their canvas, they step back and look at the blank canvas to envision what the painting will become. Christmas decorating can be thought of in the same light. Think of yourself as an artist and your home as the canvas. Picture in your mind the kind of lights you are going to use and where your lights and decorations will be placed. Have an idea in your mind as to what your finished masterpiece will look like.

When looking at your home don't look at it dead on. You want to look at it from many angles. Walk around your property and understand the landscape and make a drawing of your property including the trees, bushes and shrubs as well as your walkway and driveway. After you have it down on paper, it makes it much easier to understand where your decorations can be placed. If you are not a great artist and are more apt to use computer programs, you're in luck. A company by the name of HolidaySoft has created software made specifically for Christmas decorating. The software is called Holiday Lights Designer and allows the user to import pictures of their property and make it come to life by adding all sorts of Christmas lights and yard décor. You can add all types of lights from miniature to C-9, from net lights to icicle lights and everything in between. You can also import pre-loaded Christmas lawn decorations as well as import your own hand built Christmas decorations. But wait. There's more! After adding all the lights to your home and surroundings, you can turn the light skies to dark to see what your house will look like at night. You can add animation to make them chase and flash at different speeds and synchronize them. You can get a free 30 day trial at www.holidaysoft.com or you can purchase it for a relatively low price of $29.99. Not a bad deal if you're going to be committed to decorating your home for Christmas.

Tip: If you intend on drawing your display by hand, include any outlets on the front or back of your home in the drawing. Pencil them into the drawing as small squares on the house. Inside those squares write the number of outlets you have.

Sizing Up Your Home

After your drawing is complete, you're going to need to measure your home. This is a critical step as these measurements will give you an idea as to how many strings of lights you will need for each area you wish to decorate. Bear in mind that when shopping for the lights, the box will state "lighted length." This is important to know as most light strings have a foot to two foot lead before the first light in the string. On some applications, such as icicle lights, you want a continuous flow of lights with no "dead areas." Therefore, use the lighted length in determining the number of strings needed for a certain application. For example, after measuring your gutters, you find that the total length is 100 feet. When looking at the box of icicle lights, you notice that the ***total length*** of the light string is 12 feet long. The stated ***lighted length*** is 10 feet long. Therefore, you would need 10 strings to span 100 feet.

> ***Tip: To calculate the total number of strings you will need, divide the total number of feet by the lighted length.***

Lighting Up the Sky

For quite a few years I've taken on the daunting task of putting Christmas lights on our roof. Many people have complemented my wife and me on how nice it looks but always ask how I keep them up without them sliding off the roof. Well, it's a little easier than you think, but it takes some time to complete.

The first decision you need to make is how you want to lay the lights on the roof. If you intend to lay the lights vertically, from the front to the back of the house, then you will need to measure from the gutter in the front of the house to the peak of the roof and multiply times two. This length will determine how long the string of lights needs to be to reach from the front to the back of the house. Depending on the size of your roof, you may need more than one string of lights to run from front to back. Most light strings are 35 feet long but you can find them up to 60 feet long.

You will also need to know how far to space each string of lights. If you want each string of lights spaced one foot apart and your roof is 60 feet long, you would need 60 strings of lights. See illustration marked "Lights Vertical" at the end of this section.

> ***Tip: Remember our discussion on lighted length? If your lead is a foot in length, don't space the lights farther than 1 foot apart so that you can connect 3 strings together.***

As you lay the strings on your roof use shingle clips to hold the strings in place. For extra security zip tie the ends to gutters. Make sure that the male end of the string is facing towards the side of the house that has the outlet. This way you will eliminate the need for unwanted or excessive extension cords. To eliminate the need for multiple extension cords, use three-way adapters to connect more than one run (three light sets) to one extension cord.

If you want to run the lights horizontally, so that they follow each row of shingles, then your calculation is a little more involved. You will need to measure the roof lengthwise (from side to side) as well as vertically from the gutter to the peak. Take the total length of the roof and multiply it times the number of rows of shingles. Add the total height of the roof and this will give you the total number of feet to continuously cover the roof with lights.

For example, if your roof is 60 feet in length, has 20 rows of shingles and is 20 feet in height, you would have a total of 1,220 feet (Length x Number of Rows of Shingles + Height of Roof = Total Feet). Now that you have the total number of feet you need to cover, you'll need to know how many light strings to purchase. Before you can do the next calculation, you will need to know the length of the light string. We'll assume that a string of lights is 60 feet long. Divide the total calculated footage by the length of the light string and you will have total number of strings needed to cover the roof. In this example, our total calculated footage is 1,220 feet is 60 feet so you will need just over 20 strings of lights. See diagram marked "Lights Horizontal" at the end of this section.

Now that you have your lights, it's time to attach them to the roof. Lay the light set out with the male end pointing towards the outlet and attach them to the shingles with shingle clips spaced every couple of feet. Make sure to pull them a little taut so they don't droop too much. After you have connected three sets of lights together you will need to start a new run. Start the new run as you did the first, running an extension cord from the new run to the outlet. You may use the three-way adapter to connect these runs into one extension cord. Repeat these steps over again until the roof is finished.

While lights on the roof do look nice, you have to decide whether or not it's safe enough to be up on the roof doing this. My house is a single level ranch with a very simple pitch making it easier than most homes to safely work on the roof. Some houses may have a steeper pitch or a more complicated roof which can lead to you being injured or killed if you're not using good judgment. If you don't feel safe being on the roof, then don't do it. Better to be safe than sorry.

> ***Tip:** While the spacing between lights is a preferential choice, it can make or break a display. For a small house (single level ranch), the spacing of the lights should be at least 4 to 6 inches apart while larger homes (two stories or more) can get away with normal spacing or 2.5 inches between each bulb. Why? Normal spacing will make a smaller home look out of place and too bright but may compliment a larger home (due to the height and distance from the street level).*

Lights Vertical

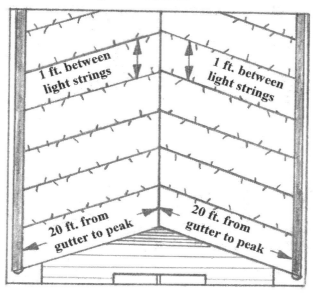

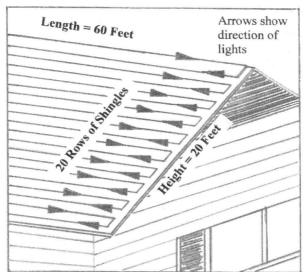

Lights Horizontal

Siding Lights

In 2007, I decided to try lighting up the entire house with lights by attaching lights to the siding of the house. This was the first year I decided to see how many lights on can get on a small ranch without it going up in flames. There were many failed attempts on getting the lights to stay on the siding until I came upon siding clips. As I described in the previous chapter on clips, they are very easy to use. Slip your siding clip under your siding spacing them about six to twelve inches apart. The pressure of the siding will help hold the clip in place. Before stringing the lights on the clips, take a step back and look at the house. Picture where the lights should start, any obstacles in the way (such as windows, shutters, etc …) and where the outlet is located. Your windows are going to be your obstacles as you don't want to string the lights across the window but around the window. Lay the lights over each clip and make sure to take up any slack as the lights tend to sag a little over time. This project is a little easier than being up on the roof and takes much less time to do. Since the clips are clear plastic, you can leave them up all year long, which makes the job of putting the lights up much easier the following year.

Tip: Just as with the roof, don't use lights spaced any less than 4 inches or your home will look too bright from the street.

Window Lighting

Lighting up the outline of a window isn't as easy as it seems. The main reason most people don't light up their windows is because they think that they need to staple a bunch lights to their windows like Chevy Chase in *Christmas Vacation*. This of course, will leave plenty of small holes to fill. In addition, you want to have your lights hung completely straight. Wind-O-Light (www.wind-o-light.com) is a great product that allows you to attach miniature lights to your windows with no fasteners while keeping the lights perfectly straight. The frames are installed from inside the house and slip into each window. Each frame is adjustable to fit any window up to 34" x 70." If your window is bigger than 34" x 70" you can still use Wind-O-Light but you would need more than one set. The sets are supplied with miniature lights that slip into the pre-drilled holes making a perfectly straight outline of the window. The best part was the ease of assembly and disassembly. That is, you don't have to disassemble them. After the season is over, remove them from your window and put them away for next year.

Trees and Bushes

Decorating the trees and bushes can add a nice visual appeal to your display. To make your bushes have uniform look and feel, I would recommend using net lighting. While you can decorate the bushes with strings of lights if wanted, net lights are easier to apply and the lights are spaced appropriately to give uniform appearance. For smaller bushes you may only need one box but bigger bushes may require two sets or more.

As for trees, stringing the lights can be a dizzying job. Starting at the base of the tree wrap the lights around the trunk spacing each wrap a couple of inches apart. Do this until the trunk is covered in lights. When you reach the branches you can continue using this method, but you'll have a lot of lights on the tree. I recommend loosely wrapping the lights around the branch, from the trunk towards the tip of the branch. Once you get to the end of the branch, follow it to the next branch and continue until all the branches are strung. Don't worry if you can't reach the very top branches as no one will really notice in the dark.

If you have a tree with a large trunk, you should consider using trunk lights. Trunk lights are designed like net lights but are meant to fit around the trunks of much bigger trees making it an easier application than winding strings of miniature lights around the trunk.

Yard Decorations

There is an overabundance of yard decorations on the market. So many, that it can make your head spin. The different types of pre-made yard decorations we will be discussing are:

- Blowmolds
- Inflatables
- Wire Frames
- Handmade Decorations

While the first three take less time to setup, handmade decorations add an "awe-factor" to your display.

Blow Molds

Blow molds have been around for many years. Some blow molds dating back 30, 40 even 50 years, can fetch a pretty penny. A blow mold is a hollow plastic decoration molded into figures and other objects such as candles, soldiers and even nativity scenes. Some of these blow molds take regular household incandescent bulbs (upwards of 60W) and others take C7 bulbs to light them up. One of the downfalls of the blow molds is that they aren't as appealing to the eye as they once were and they have a tendency to fall over if not properly secured. Since they are hollow, they can be secured in a variety of ways. Some can be filled with sand to make the base steady or you can use a brick or two in the bottom to keep them still. For smaller blow molds, you can cut rebar to size and place them over the rebar. Some people like them because they are easy to put up and take down but personally, I have decided not to use them anymore as they tend to take up a lot of storage space.

Inflatables

One of the more recent inventions in decorating is the advent of the inflatable. These decorations are made with water-resistant nylon, come in a variety of different characters and are made for many different holidays. I have a 6 foot turkey for my front lawn that I put up during Thanksgiving. While that turkey may have almost cost me my marriage, he is liked by all the children in my neighborhood and is appropriately named Mr. Gobbles.

Setting up the inflatable is very easy and takes about 10 minutes. The inflatable is attached to a base with a fan. The base is secured to the ground with lawn stakes that are supplied with each inflatable. Each inflatable comes with tie-downs that attach to pre-sewn hooks on the inflatable.

These tie-downs are then attached to lawn stakes to keep the inflatable from blowing over in the wind. Once the base and the inflatable are secure, plug it into your outlet and the fan will inflate your decoration.

As for seeing the inflatable at night, companies install a series of C-7 bulbs inside each inflatable. These bulbs, should they burn out can be replaced with a standard C-7 bulb. Also, unlike a string of lights, these decorations take a 5 amp fuse. I like to have additional 5 amp fuses on hand as they do tend to burn out after awhile. Not to worry, they are easily replaced and the instructions supplied with each inflatable will tell you where the fuse is located and how to replace it.

> ***Tip: Before securing the inflatable to the ground, inflate it so that you can see which way it is facing. Then you can adjust it and stake it to the ground.***

Wire Frames

You may not know what they are called but I'm sure you've seen them around your neighborhood. If you've seen a lighted deer on the front lawn then you've seen a wire frame decoration. These decorations are made from steel wire, molded and welded together to form a design. Once the design is complete, lights are attached. They come completely assembled in the box and are easy to setup. All you need to do is stake them to the ground and plug them in. Some of them fold up so that you can store them flat.

Holographic wire frames are another type that you may have seen in the stores at Christmas. These yard decorations have wire frames but have a holographic plastic image attached to them. You can find just about any character known to man made into a Christmas wire frame display.

Handmade Displays

If you can make your displays by hand, the display takes on a life of its own because you can say that YOU built it! Over the years, I have used everything from blow molds, to inflatables and even wire frames. Slowly, my display is turning into a display built completely by hand. Of course, there are some pre-built yard decorations, like the wire frame deer, that I will continue to use because it's easier to buy them than build them. But for the most part, 90% of the display is my own design and inspiration. This transformation from a 90% commercial display to 90% hand built display did not happen overnight. Each year I decided to work on a different project and before I knew it, I was eliminating some of the commercial stuff that I'd bought over the years. You can do the same but start off small and work your way up! Before you know it, you'll have an all hand built display as well.

The following are all decorations that you can build with supplies from the local home store. They are very easy to build and will compliment your display.

Driveway Arches

The first year I decided to put arches over the driveway, my neighbors were confused. They asked me if I was extending the garage over the driveway. I said, "Nope, just putting up some arches for the Christmas display." I think everyone in my neighborhood thought I was out of my mind. But, you know what? The arches turned out great and everyone loved them.

The arches are made out of 1 ¼ inch Schedule 40 electrical PVC. Do not buy plumbing PVC. Plumbing PVC is rigid and does not bend. Electrical PVC is flexible and has a flared end on one side allowing you to connect one piece to the other.

Other material you will need:

- 24 feet of ½ inch rebar (comes in 12 foot lengths)
- green spray paint
- nylon rope
- one inch screw eyes
- silicone caulk
- automotive grease
- Christmas lights (approximately 1,000 per arch)
- garland (approximately 100 feet per arch)
- general purpose metal cutting blade for a chop saw or bi-metal blades for a reciprocating saw

Excluding the lights, the approximate cost of this project is $40.00.

Before you begin, you will need to make a small calculation to figure out how many feet of PVC is needed to make one arch. I'm going to let you in on a secret. I flunked math three times in college, but I do remember this calculation for some odd reason. Since the arches will span the driveway, you will need to calculate the dimension of half a circle (180 degrees) to give you the total footage of PVC per arch. Measure the width of your driveway, divide by 2 and multiply times 3.14 (Pi for those who are not mathematically inclined).

To illustrate this with numbers, let's look at my driveway. My driveway is 26 feet in width; 26 divided by 2 = 13. This gives you the height of the arch in feet. Multiply 13 times 3.14 and that will give me 40.86 feet. This tells me that I will need 40 feet of PVC per arch. Luckily enough, PVC comes in 10 foot lengths. But what happens when your final calculation is not a round number? Not to worry. If you have an odd number as your final calculation (such as 37 feet) you would still need 40 feet of PVC but you would only use three 10 foot lengths and cut the fourth length to seven feet.

Now that you have your measurements, you need to decide how many arches you are going to build. If you've ever bought flowers, you know that an odd number of flowers look better in a vase than an even number. The same holds true for your arches. Knowing that you want an odd number of arches evenly spaced, measure the length of your driveway and divide by the number of arches you want to build. For example, my driveway is a little over 27 feet long. Since I am looking for an odd number of arches this was easy. Every nine feet there would be an arch for a total of three arches. If each arch for my driveway required 40 feet of PVC, and I'm building three arches, I would need a total of 120 feet of PVC.

The PVC is usually a hideous gray color so I recommend painting them. A nice technique is to paint them forest green (or a darker green color) and before you wrap lights around each arch, attach garland. This way, the garland and arches will blend together in the daylight making the arches more eye-catching.

Before you can start wrapping lights or garland around your arches, you'll need to get them assembled. Lay your lengths of PVC on the ground, grease the inside of each flared end and insert the next length of PVC until all lengths for that arch are connected. Repeat this process until each arch is assembled. The reason for the grease is so your sections can be easily disconnected at the end of the season. Without the grease, the sections would freeze together making it impossible to disconnect.

Now that your arches are assembled, you'll need to cut two pieces of rebar for each arch. Cutting the rebar may be a little difficult if you don't have the proper tools. You can cut the rebar with a reciprocating saw supplied with a bi-metal blade but you will use many blades due to the hardness of the rebar. An easier method would be to use a chop saw installed with a general purpose metal cutting blade. Remember to use proper eye, face and body protection when cutting the rebar as there will be many sparks. After cutting the rebar, dip it into cold water to cool the cut ends so that you don't burn your hands.

Each section of rebar should be four feet long as they will be pounded, at a slight angle, 1 ½ feet into the ground. After you have your rebar cut, measure your driveway lengthwise from the starting point of where you want the first arch placed. Space each section of rebar equally apart from one another on each side of the driveway leaving extra room to tie off the arches on both ends. For example, if your driveway is 30 feet long, and you are planning to have three arches, space the rebar 9 feet apart on either side of the driveway. You may need to make adjustments based on your particular situation. Once all your rebar is in the ground, it is time to raise the arches.

Depending on the size of your arch, this may be a two person job. Take one end of the arch and slide it over a section of rebar and walk the other end of the arch across the driveway until you can slide it over the second section of rebar. Repeat this process until all of your arches are up.

In order to keep them from falling over, you will need to tie them down. One method to secure them is to tie the arches to the garage. Drill two holes into the garage so they line up with the arches. Coat the screw eyes with silicone caulk and insert into each hole. The caulk will give you protection against water damage to your home. Tie a nylon rope to one of the screw eyes and stretch the rope to the first arch. Wrap the rope once around the first arch and repeat for the next arches. Once you've wrapped the last arch, pull the nylon rope down towards the ground and wrap it around a piece of rebar in front of the last arch. Cap it with a piece of PVC so that no one gets hurt. Your arches are now secure and you can get on with the fun part ... wrapping the lights!

While the garland does take time, it is a very nice touch. Before wrapping the lights, wrap garland around each arch and zip tie the garland every 12 to 24 inches. After the garland is up, wrap the arches with lights in the same fashion. Remember to keep the male end of the plug for each arch facing towards the outlet. As for the color of the lights, use your imagination and have fun.

Arches

Miniature Trees

By far, the easiest decoration to build for your display, are miniature trees. They are fun to build and are a great summer project for the kids on rainy days.

To build one tree, you will need:
- Floral easel
- 300 miniature lights
- Lots of zip ties

Excluding the lights, the approximate cost of this project is $5.00 per tree.

At first, I didn't know what a floral easel was until I went into a craft store. Ask anyone in the store, and they should be able to point you in the right direction. If you have a hard time finding the easel, your local garden store might have a pyramid shaped tomato cage.

When you stand the easel up you'll notice that two of its legs will be longer than third making the tree stand at an angle. Take a pair of wire clippers and snip an appropriate length off the longer legs to make the easel stand straight.

Drop the female end of the light string into the top of the easel and zip tie it at the top (the highest point). As you wind the lights around the entire easel, apply zip-ties after each pass. Once you are done, repeat the process with the second and third string applying zip-ties sporadically. Don't forget to connect the male ends of the second and third string to the female end of the first string. This way you will have one plug at the bottom of the tree which will connect to the extension cord.

These trees are great for outlining your property and "planting" around the mega trees we're going to build next. Also, storing them couldn't be easier. The trees can be stacked one on top of the other thereby using up very little storage space. Be careful when stacking though, as you do run the risk of breaking the bulbs if you force them on top of each other.

> ***Tip: To make life a little easier, place the easel on a Lazy Susan and spin it while wrapping the lights.***

Mega Trees

The little trees we just built only stand about two feet tall. But how about a tree for your front yard that will astound the neighbors and tower 10 or 20 feet tall? That's right, mega trees, as the name implies are trees that stand over 10 feet tall. While they take a little time to build, I've found that they are an awesome addition to a display and you get a great workout going up and down a ladder for two or three hours.

To build a 10 foot tree, you will need the following materials:

- 10 foot length of 1 ¼ inch electrical conduit
- 10 foot length of 1 inch electrical conduit
- 20 feet of ½ inch electrical PVC

- Circular electrical cover plate (about 4 inches in diameter)
- 8 feet of rebar
- (40) 3/8th inch fender washers
- 3/8th inch threaded rod 12 inches long
- (3) 3/8th inch nuts
- (8) clothesline hooks with 2 nuts per hook
- Zip ties
- Approximately 2,500 lights

Excluding the lights, the approximate cost of this project is $50.00

Before we begin assembling the tree, we must build the tree topper (see picture of assembled tree topper at the end of this section). The tree topper will allow us to string our lights to the top and provide a place for us to hang them. To build the tree topper, drill eight holes in the electrical cover plate. Make sure that they are evenly spaced and closer to the edge. Those holes should be the same diameter of your clothesline bolts. In the center of the plate, drill a hole the same diameter of your threaded rod.

Tip: Before drilling the holes make sure you wear gloves to protect your hands from burning. To prevent any "break-through" on the opposite side of the metal plate, place a piece of wood or extra metal underneath the

electrical plate. If you do have some "break-through" it can be filed or grinded off.

Take the clothes line bolts and insert one into each hole. Thread one nut so that it is secured to the bottom of the plate and the other to the top of the plate. This will keep the bolt from moving around too much. Repeat this with the next seven bolts. After all the bolts are attached, feed the threaded rod through the center hole and attach with a nut. Slide the 40 fender washers on the bottom of the threaded rod and secure the bottom with a wing nut. These washers act as a weight to keep the tree topper upright. With the tree topper assembled, we can now work on building the rest of the tree.

Cut the one inch diameter electrical conduit down to seven feet and drive it two feet into the ground leaving five feet exposed. Before driving it into the ground make sure there are no obstructions (such as a sprinkler system) and it is as level as possible. This piece will hold the 1 ¼ inch electrical conduit upright. Attach your tree topper to one end of the 10 foot, 1 ¼ inch electrical conduit and slip the entire 10 foot section over the piece you just drove into the ground. You now have the trunk of the tree. Since we are making a 10 foot tree, there's no need to tie it down as it will hold up quite well even in the worst of storms. If you do want to build a mega tree bigger than 10 feet tall, I would recommend tying it down with guy wire.

Now that we have the trunk and tree topper built, we need to build the base. The base will serve as a place to tie off the lights which forms our tree. Take the two sections of 10 foot, ½ inch electrical PVC and connect them together to make a circle. This should look like one really big hula hoop. Once we make our big hula hoop, it will give us a circle that is five feet in diameter. The diameter of the base should equal half of the height of the tree.

To support the base off the ground, your rebar needs to be cut in two foot lengths. Place the base around the trunk then drive the rebar into the ground inside the base and zip-tie the base one inch from the top of the rebar.

Before you start stringing up the lights, you have to supply the tree with a power source. Since you will be using almost 2,500 lights, you're going to need an adapter that can handle more than one extension cord. At the home stores you can find three outlet lawn stakes that work very well for this application. You'll need at least two of them as well as some three outlet adapters to connect all the light strings. Attach the three multi-outlet lawn stakes to the trunk using the zip ties positioning them closer to the top of the tree.

Tip: Make sure to look at the maximum amperage of the three outlet lawn stake. Not all of them can handle the same electrical load.

Start at the top of the tree connecting the light string to the multi-outlet and pass it over one of the clothesline hooks. Bring the light string down to the outside of the base and wrap the light string around and back up again.

Continue doing this until all light strings are up. To keep a uniform appearance, space the light strings four inches apart and zip tie them to the base.

> *Tip: Before stringing up lights in any project, test each string prior to using. This way you'll make sure all the lights are in working order. Sometimes you get a dud of a string!*

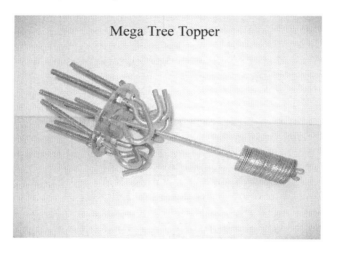
Mega Tree Topper

Signs and Plywood Cutouts

Buying a product from a store can satisfy you for a little while, but making something by hand can satisfy you for a lifetime. As my display starts to grow, I've found different and interesting ways to add hand-built decorations other than the mega tree, arches or little trees. Some hand-built lawn decorations, such as the plywood cutouts we will be making, are very easy to build and assemble. These lawn decorations are fashioned by cutting the display out of ½ inch plywood with a jigsaw. Most plans require one sheet of plywood making it a relatively inexpensive project to make. You can search the internet and find a ton of patterns ranging from deer to nativity scenes to signs. One manufacturer that has a very nice selection is The Winfield Collection. Their patterns are very easy to follow and have lawn decorations not only for Christmas, but for most holidays. You can find them on the internet at www.thewinfieldcollection.com.

One type of yard decoration that can be built from plywood is holiday signs. Holiday signs are made by individually cutting each letter from plywood to make sayings such as Merry Christmas, Joy, Noel, or even Santa Land Here. An on-line company called Wood Craft Plans (www.woodcraftplans.com) sells alphabet stencils up to two feet tall. In addition to selling the stencils, they also have tracing paper available that fits four by eight sheets of plywood.

We will be looking at how to build a sign that reads, "Keep Christ in Christmas."

The materials you will need to complete this project are:

- 3 full sheets of plywood (4 foot by 8 foot) a ½ inch thick
- outdoor latex paint
- approximately 2,200 lights

- 13/64th drill bit
- jigsaw
- drill
- silicone caulk

Excluding the lights, the approximate cost of this project is $50.00

The first step in building the sign is to take a look at what letters repeat themselves. In Keep Christ in Christmas the E, C, I, S, H, R and T repeat. Why is this important? Well, this will save us some time. Instead of cutting each letter out separately, you can stack cut the letters that repeat. To stack cut letters, stack as many plywood blanks as you need to cut the repeating letters (if you have two C's you'll need two blanks) and secure the stack by driving a brad nail into each corner. Transfer the pattern to the wood by placing the transfer paper between your pattern and the wood and you're ready to cut out your letter.

After all the letters are cut, it's time to decide how to attach the lights. In this design, the lights are fed from the back of each letter through pre-drilled holes with a 13/64th drill bit and secured with a little dab of silicone caulk. Before we can go crazy and start drilling hundreds of holes in our freshly cut letters, you need to know how many to drill. You will find that different letters will take a different number of lights. For example, the letter "K" has more area to cover than the letter "I" therefore it will require more lights. Try to space the lights at least one inch apart and about a half inch from the edge of the letter to have a uniform look. On the letter "K" that might mean 100 lights, but the "I" may only take 50. Mark the letters with a pencil as to the location of the holes before you start drilling. Just as we stack cut the repetitive letters, you can "stack drill" them as well. Once all the holes are drilled, sand down the letters with 100 grit sand paper. Now the letters are ready to be painted and assembled. Paint them prior to assembling the lights and let them dry. To assemble the lights, slip each miniature light into the holes that you've drilled and add a little dab of silicone to hold them in place. In this Keep Christ in Christmas display, all the letters had white lights except for the word Christ. The word Christ was made out of blue lights and blink to draw more attention to the meaning. Use your imagination and make your own!

As for standing them up in yard, well, they're not going to stand up by themselves. To properly secure them mount a two foot piece of rebar to the back of each letter. If you're using ½ inch rebar, mount them to the back with ½ inch electrical conduit fasteners.

> ***Tip: To save on the amount of rebar, you can attach the letters together with small pieces of angle iron on the top and bottom of each letter to spell out an entire word. This way you'd only need a couple pieces of rebar and you can move the whole word instead of individual letters, taking less time to set up.***

Back of Sign Letters

Front of Sign Letters

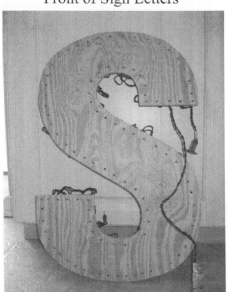

Decorative Fence

Another addition to your display that is very easy to build is a decorative fence for around your yard. Not only is it visually appealing and easy to put up and tear down, but it also acts as a barrier to keep people off of your property. That's not to say that I don't want people admiring the lights. I just don't want people accidentally tripping over extension cords and injuring themselves.

To make the fence you will need:

- Rebar (cut into four foot lengths)
- ¾ inch PVC cut into three foot lengths (plumbing not electrical)
- Spray paint (color of your choice)
- Miniature lights

Excluding the lights, the approximate cost of this project is $50.00

The PVC in this plan is different than what has been previously discussed. This plan calls for the use of <u>plumbing</u> PVC instead of electrical PVC. Since the PVC is being used as our fence posts, we need a material that is rigid. Plumbing PVC is very rigid, whereas electrical PVC is more flexible.

The other differences from previous plans are the lengths of rebar and lights and you will need. These lengths will be determined by the length of the fence. Let's assume that the fence in this example will be 60 feet long.

The spacing of each fence post is up to you, but for purposes of this plan, they are spaced three feet apart. To determine how many fence posts you'll need, divide the number of feet in your fence by the spacing of each fence post. If our fence is going to be 60 feet long and we're spacing the posts three feet apart, we would need 20 fence posts (60 divided by 3 = 20).

Now that we know how many fence posts we'll need, we'll have to cut the PVC and rebar to the appropriate lengths. The length of the fence posts will differ from the length of the rebar. According to the material list above, the fence posts should be three feet tall and the rebar should be 4 feet tall. The rebar must be longer than the PVC because it will be will be driven 1 foot into the ground to support the fence posts. Therefore, if you need 20 fence posts and 20 pieces of rebar, you would need to purchase 60 feet of PVC (20 posts at three feet tall) and 80 feet of rebar (20 pieces of rebar four feet tall).

Since the amount of PVC and rebar can vary depending on your area of coverage remember these helpful calculations:

- Measure the length in feet that the fence will span.
- Length of fence **DIVIDED** by the spacing between each post = number of fence posts
- Number of fence posts or rebar **TIMES** the height of the fence post/rebar = length of PVC/rebar needed.

Painting the PVC isn't required, but it does add a nice aesthetic look to the fence instead of plain white posts sticking out of the ground. Spray paint them any color you wish and get creative with them. You can candy stripe them, wrap garland around them or sprinkle glitter on them right after spraying them with paint.

The very last step before assembly is to cut a ¼ inch notch in the top of each piece PVC approximately 1 inch in depth. This notch will hold the lights in place when stringing them from post to post.

Now we are ready to assemble. Starting at one end of your property, pound the first piece of rebar into the ground so that it sticks up about 36 inches. Do this for all the rebar spacing them according to your calculations.

Tip: Lay the rebar on the ground spaced appropriately apart for your display before driving each piece into the grass. Take the first and last piece and pound them into the ground. Run a level line from those two pieces. The line is your guide for the remaining pieces so they are level and the same height.

After all the rebar is in the ground, slide one piece of PVC over each piece of rebar and you're ready to start assembling the lights.

The lights will swag from one post to the next and are only wrapped on the first and last post. Start with the male end of your light string at the bottom of the first post and wrap the light up and around the post and through the pre-cut notch at the top. Swag the lights from one post to the other until you reach the end. Once you reach the last post, wrap the lights down that post and you're done!

You're probably thinking, how many lights do I need? If you your swag is one foot deep and your posts are three feet apart, you'd need approximately four feet of lights between each post. In our example we have 20 posts. Therefore, we would need more than 80 feet of lights. When purchasing your lights, know the length you are trying to cover and buy strings that are greater than or equal to that length.

Hopefully I have given you some ideas for your display. Take these ideas and make them your own. Remember, the arches, fences, and plywood cutouts can be difficult to make and are time consuming. Start these in the summer months so you can build them outside and enjoy the fresh air. Once these projects have been built, they only require routine maintenance.

As the years go by you will find that it will take you less time to assemble your display. The first time I put lights on the roof, it took over six hours to complete. Now, it takes about 3 ½ hours for the whole roof. I've learned short cuts, gained more experience and know my work pace. The more times you assemble your display, the less time it will take you to finish. It may seem like a lot of work in the beginning, but the sense of accomplishment and admiration from others is pure enjoyment!

Chapter 5

Snakes in the Grass

If your display is starting to look like *Christmas Vacation* and people refer to you as Clark Griswold, you may have an obsession with Christmas lights. Well, if that's the case, then you probably have many, and I mean MANY, extension cords. You can easily wind up with thousands of feet in extension cords all over the lawn. However, you don't want it to be a jumbled mess, especially if you are having problems with a part of your display and need to find the root of the problem.

Running the extension cords from the decorations to the outlets will be one of the more daunting tasks to perform. One product that can make your job easier and eliminate the use of multiple extension cords is the multiple outlet lawn stake. These three outlet adapters have a screw-on lawn stake and a long extension cord that makes it easy to connect multiple extension cords to one outlet. Not every manufacturer rates their outlets at the same amperage. Make sure you know how many amps the three outlet adapter is capable of handling before plugging in all your lights. They are marked with an amp rating that can be found in the instructions, on the box or the unit.

> ***Tip:** Some of these lawn stakes come with timers that turn the lights on and off at a set time. While this can be an economical purchase, they don't always work in unison. Because different areas of you lawn may get different amounts of sunlight, there is the possibility that one area of your display will be on while another area is off.*

Tag Your Ends

After everything is connected and you have the extension cords running to each outlet, label each cord. Take a piece of shipping tape and wrap a good five to six inch section around the neck of the extension cord at the outlet. With an indelible marker, write what you have running on that particular cord (for example, if your arches are running off one extension cord, mark it "ARCHES"). This way, if you do have any problems, you can easily locate the source.

One of the major problems you will encounter will be moisture. Moisture is our enemy during the Christmas season (as are vandals, but that's another chapter). Since you are most likely plugging your lights into GFI's, you will encounter periodic outages due to moisture on the plug connections. GFI's, as we discussed in the first chapter, are also more sensitive to condensation and therefore, trip more often. But then again, isn't that their job? While I can't promise that some of these techniques will cure the problem 100% of the time, they will lessen the number of times your lights will be out.

Prop Up Your Ends

One of the biggest water-related problems you'll encounter is the accumulation of water around the connections between the extension cords and your lights. The collection of water or snow is one of the main reasons GFI's trip. To solve this problem, stake the electrical connections up off the ground with bamboo tomato stakes and zip ties.

> *Tip: Cut the bamboo into one foot lengths and stake them six to 8 inches off the ground. This will keep them above any small puddles or snowfalls you should happen to have.*

Cover Your Ends

One trick that many have talked about is wrapping your electrical connections with plastic wrap and duct taping both ends. While this sounds like a great idea it actually doesn't keep moisture out. Wrapping the ends can produce condensation and cause the GFI to trip. If you want to take an extra step to prevent your GFI from tripping, cover all your staked connections with a freezer bag. Loosely placing a freezer bag over the staked connections will keep out rain and snow and allow air to flow around the connection eliminating condensation.

Other than covering your entire display with a tarp when it rains or snows, there is not much that you can do. With a little luck, these little tricks will help prevent from it happening all the time.

Chapter 6
Watts Up With You?

You've got everything up. The extension cords have been run to the outlets. The breaker trips. You've overloaded the circuit.

This is a very common mistake to make when connecting your lights to the outlets. Knowing a little something about the capacity of your breakers and how much power those little lights are drawing will minimize the likelihood of this ever happening again.

First and foremost let me begin by reinforcing the need to hire a professional electrician. It's not worth doing it yourself to save a few dollars only to have someone get injured or killed. Make sure it's done right so that you can have a safe and Merry Christmas!

Most of your circuits, whether you have breakers or fuses, will have either 15 amp or 20 amp load capacity. This means that breakers can handle a load of up to 15 or 20 amps depending on which breaker or fuse is installed. For breakers or fuses running a continuous current (such as one on a non-animated "static display"), you never want to use more than 80% of your breaker's maximum amperage. If you do, at some point the breaker will trip due to overloading. To determine the maximum capacity of your circuit breaker, take 80% of the total amperage of the breaker. This will give you the maximum number of amps you can safely run on the breaker. For example, a 20 amp breaker can run 16 amps and a 15 amp breaker can run 12 amps.

Determining Total Amperage

Since I mainly use miniature lights and C7's, that is what I will be illustrating. These calculations can be done with any type of lights from LED's to C9's and even inflatables. All you need to know is the amount of amps the light or decoration is drawing.

Next to LED lights, miniature lights use very little power. The miniature light sets we will discuss are strings of 100 and 70 lights. The 100 light set is marked at 0.34 amps per string. The 70 light set is marked at 0.40 amps per string. At first it seems a little odd for fewer lights to have more amps. The reason why? The 70 light set takes 3.5 volt lights which are brighter than the typical 2.5 volt light bulb found on most miniature lights and therefore, draws more power. Don't think that just because there are fewer lights on a string that you will use less power. Some manufacturers can vary the amount of amperage a set takes.

To calculate the amount of lights that may be used on one circuit, follow these directions:

- As discussed in the previous section, take 80% of the total load of your circuit breaker (for example, 80% of a 20 amp circuit breaker equals 16 amps).
- Divide 16 amps by the amperage of one string and this will give you the total number of strings that may be put on one circuit (for example, 16 amps divided by 0.34 amps per string gives you 47 strings).

The following is a breakdown as to how many strings may be connected to one outlet depending on their string amperage:

> 533   60 light LED (mini look-a-like) set at 0.03 amps per string
> 47   100 light miniature set at 0.34 amps per string
> 40   70 light miniature set at 0.40 amps per string
> 15   25 light C7 set at 1.04 amps per string
> (All based on 80% of 20 amp circuit)

You're probably thinking, all this information is great, but how am I supposed to know how many amps I have connected to a particular outlet? With all these lights it can get a little overwhelming. You will need to keep track of how many light strings, the kind of light strings and the amperage of each string you are running to a breaker. This may sound like a Herculean task, but is quite simple. Keep all "like" sets of lights running off the same outlet (i.e. all miniature lights or all C7's). Once you know how many light sets you have running to the outlet, multiply the amperage of one set by the total number of light sets. This will give you a general idea as to the total amount of amperage. If you are uncertain as to the amperage of the light set, you can find that information on the box the lights came in, in the directions or on the collar of the set itself. Don't forget that amperage can vary from set to set depending on the manufacturer, therefore don't assume that the amps will be the same.

Amperage will also change depending on the number of lights in a string as well as the type of light being used. Light sets with 100 lights in a string will draw more amps than a set with 50 lights in a string. C7's and C9's will draw much more power than an LED or miniature light. These factors must be taken into consideration when running your lights to the outlet.

> ***Tip: Remember to connect "like" set to "like" set. Don't commingle different types of lights (such as C7's and miniature lights, etc ...) on the same run.***

Now that I've taught you the difficult way to calculate the total amperage of your lights, let's look at a gadget that will make your life a lot easier-the Kill-O-Watt. This device can be found online at www.p3international.com and in stores and is made by P3 International. The Kill-O-Watt can tell you how many amps your lights are drawing as well as how many amps your electrical appliances throughout the house are drawing. The Kill-O-Watt not only helps you at Christmas, but can help you save money all year long by showing you the power appliances are using even if they aren't on. That's right! An appliance doesn't have to be on to draw power. To use the Kill-O-Watt, plug it into the outlet and plug your Christmas lights into the Kill-O-Watt device. It will tell you the total number of amps you are using. While you can pretty much trust the device to give you an accurate number, you should know how many strings you can run to an outlet for each string type you own. Use the Kill-O-Watt to double check yourself and your numbers. As long as you follow the rule of threes, use GFI's, know your numbers and treat electricity with respect, things should go just fine during the Christmas season.

Chapter 7

Protect Yourself!

I've always loved *Frosty the Snowman*. *Frosty the Snowman* was, and still is, my favorite cartoon during the Christmas season. I don't know what it is, but every time Frosty melts, it brings a tear to my eye, even though I know he comes back to life.

The one year that I decided to add inflatables to my display, I purchased a Grinch, and of course, Frosty. One night after I turned on the display, I noticed that the Grinch and Frosty had not inflated. I went outside to check on them and they were dead. Someone had taken a knife and sliced both of them open. It felt like someone had done the same to me. I couldn't believe someone could be that cruel, especially during the Christmas season. That's when I realized that you need to protect yourself from vandals, even during Christmas.

Sure, for the most part people do tend to treat each other nicer during the Christmas season, but there's always a bad apple in the bunch to spoil it for everyone. Because of this, I looked at ways to distract people from harming the Christmas display.

Placement of Decorations

The placement of your decorations can deter or attract a vandal to your home. When you are placing your decorations on your lawn make sure that they are about six to eight feet from the curb. Keeping your decorations further in from the street will deter most vandals. Anyone looking to do harm to a display will damage things that are easily accessible (such as curbside decorations). That's where Frosty and the Grinch were located-curbside.

Signage

You wouldn't think that a small sign would do a lot of good, but it does. Consider the following signs: "Danger, High Voltage" or "This area is being monitored by closed caption television." The normal reaction to seeing these signs is to stay away. While not 100% effective, these signs will keep most people away and is the least expensive option to keep vandals off your property.

Closed Caption Television Cameras

Even if you were to add guard dogs and a sniper on the roof, you may still end up with someone doing damage to your display. It's inevitable as we are a target for people who have nothing better to do with their time. The best way to protect yourself is to install closed circuit television cameras on your property. When choosing a camera, look for an outdoor, weather resistant camera that has night vision. These cameras are readily available in the market and run about $70. One company in particular is Q-See (www.q-see.com). Q-See makes closed circuit monitors and cameras that can be used in a variety of different applications.

One application that I have found useful is to hook the camera up to a VCR and record your display for a few hours after you turn the lights off. You probably won't have any problems when the display is on. It is when the lights go out (and the bars let out) that you tend to have more problems. Place the camera at a good angle where you can view most of your display. Should anything get damaged, you'll have it on tape and can present that as evidence to your local police department. The combination of signage on your lawn and having a security camera will make the vandals think twice about harming your display.

Tip: In addition to a regular camera you can add a fake one to a different part of your display. The vandals won't know which one is real and which one is the fake.

Chapter 8

Tear Down and Storage

It's such a sad time. Christmas is over. The tree is brown and has lost most of its needles, New Year's Day has passed and you've gained 20 pounds. Now you have to take down the decorations that you put up just over a month ago. It's all so depressing. On the bright side, it is easier taking everything down than it is putting it up.

Weather

Weather plays a huge part in planning the tear down of the display. If you're lucky enough to live in a part of the country that gets fairly decent weather during the winter months then you shouldn't have a problem tearing down the display. If you're like me and live in an area that gets cold weather, snow and ice, you may have to wait a while before tearing down the display. One year I had to wait until March 17th to take down the display.

Working around the snow and ice is very difficult and dangerous. You don't want to be standing on a ladder in the snow. Let's not forget what happened to Clark Griswold in

Christmas Vacation. You should wait until the snow and ice melts before tearing down the display.

The other major obstacle you'll face is the difficulty of wrapping light strings and extension cords. Your cords will become rigid due to the cold weather. Think of your garden hose. During winter it's very stiff and hard to wrap, but in the summer, it's very elastic and easy to roll up. If you can wait until the weather warms up, it will be much easier to roll your extension cords and light strings.

Tip: Try to not dismantle any light strings in the cold weather as the miniature bulbs are much more fragile in the cold.

Storing Light Strings

There are many different ways you can wrap up your light sets after the Christmas season is over. The best way I've found to wrap lights is to wrap them in balls. Think of the way someone wraps yarn in a ball. Start by holding on to one end of the light string and wrap the lights around your hand forming a ball. It's the same technique. By wrapping them in a ball they won't get tangled with the other light strings which will save you quite a bit of time when you remove them from their storage bins.

Storing Extension Cords

Extension cords can take up an awful lot of space. Not to mention that more than a few of them together can get quite heavy. You can store them on shelves, but you'll notice that year after year, they tend to multiply. The more lights you add, the more extension cords you'll need. The easiest way to clean up the tangled mess of extension cords is to buy a wheeled garbage can. Roll up the extension cords and place them in the garbage can. This way they'll be out of your way and when you need them, you can roll the can around your property. This will save your back and the time it would take for you to carry them to your destination.

As for the rest of the display, you're going to need room. Make sure you have space reserved either in the attic, garage or basement for the Christmas decorations. If you have decorations that fold up, fold them up. You'll have a lot more room that way. Labeling your boxes is extremely important. Unless you're a member of the MENSA Society, you're not going to remember what was in each and every box. Label each box appropriately for what is stored inside. If a certain box has lights for your arches, then label it "Lights for Arches." By labeling your boxes and keeping your display organized in the off season, it will be easier and much more fun to put them all back up next year.

Chapter 9
Good Lights Gone Bad

Occasionally, you will have a set of lights go bad. More often than not, those lights can be fixed. The most common problem is having bulbs burn out. This is easily repaired by replacing the blown out bulb with a new one supplied to you by the manufacturer. These are usually found in a tiny plastic bag taped to the end of the string of lights. You can also purchase replacement bulbs at any store that sells Christmas lights.

Another common problem is having only half a string of lights work while the other half remains unlit. Most people waste money on buying a replacement set even though this problem is fixable. You just need to understand how a set of Christmas lights works.

Older style lights are wired in a series. Wiring lights in a series means that each light is wired to the next one. If one light burns out, all the lights stop working. The other way lights can be wired is in parallel. This means that if one light goes out then the others remain lit. This doesn't explain why miniature lights stay on when they are wired as a series. It's an ancient Chinese secret, but I'll share it with you anyways.

If you were to look very closely at a miniature bulb's filament, you will notice a very small piece of metal wrapped around the base. This is called the shunt. The shunt allows the current to run from one light to another even when one light burns out. If the shunt breaks or burns out, all the lights after that bad shunt will stop working, but all the lights prior to the bad shunt remain lit. Here we have our problem. We need to find the bulb with the bad shunt. Unless you have Superman's x-ray vision, you will not be able to locate the bad shunt. You could try removing each bulb until you find the bad one, but that'll take too much time.

One tool that I've found extremely helpful is the LightKeeper Pro (www.lightkeeperpro.com), an all-in-one light/fuse tester. It operates on a few watch batteries and fixes the lights by sending an electrical charge through the bad shunt temporarily fixing the set. All the lights will light up except for the bad bulb. Replace the bad bulb and "Voila!" The light set is fixed. One year I was able to fix approximately 10 to 15 bad strings. At $5.00 a string, it would have cost me upwards of $75 for new strings. The LightKeeper Pro costs about $15.00, but you'll have it forever and it will save you a lot of time and money. I highly recommend it as a worthwhile investment if you are going to start decorating for Christmas.

The fuse is the last thing you should have to worry about. Miniature lights have two small 3 amp fuses housed in the male end of the plug. The only time you really have to worry about a fuse blowing is if you disregard the Rule of 3's. If you disregard this rule, you may find yourself changing the fuses as they tend to burn out due to overheating. If you feel that the fuses are the culprit, you can check them to see if they are fully functional on your LightKeeper Pro.

Chapter 10
Get Known! Websites and Fundraising

Your display is built and everyone loves it. Don't you wish more people could see it, like friends and family in other parts of the country or world? Heck, I communicate with someone who lives in Surrey, British Columbia, Canada and I'm in Milford, Connecticut. There is no better way to do this than to set up your own website. It is a great project to work on after the Christmas season.

If you look online for web hosting services, you'll find there are many different companies offering such a service. You want a company that is reliable but one that is very easy to use. One company that we use for our website, www.thathouseinmilford.com, is Freewebs (www.freewebs.com). Freewebs allows you to setup your website free of charge with no hidden costs. They have a variety of web templates from which to choose, ranging from holiday to professional themes. The package that they offer for free gives you limited bandwidth and storage capacity. If you expect a lot of online traffic and want to store a lot of graphics, videos and pictures, then you may want to take advantage of their optional packages. They offer three different packages: Starter, Advanced and Pro. These packages offer bandwidths that range from 5GB to 100GB, storage capacities that range from 300MB to 2,500MB, up to 15 email addresses and the ability to create your own domain name for a relatively small price. Better yet, your site is ad free so you never have to subject your visitors to unwanted advertising.

Once you have your website up and running, you may want to consider doing some fundraising and make your Christmas display shine brighter than ever by helping out those less fortunate. Before you choose a cause for a fundraiser, you need to ask yourself, "What matters most to me? Who do I want to help and why?"

Let me tell you a story about how I became active in helping those in need. It was Christmas, 1981. My parents took me to New York City to see *42nd Street* on Broadway. After the show was over, we walked back to Grand Central Station. It was a little cold and there was some snow on the ground. Since we made it back to Grand Central with time to spare, my father gave me $3.00 to buy myself a pretzel and Coke. There was nothing like a New York style pretzel from Zaro's Bagels in Grand Central. I anxiously walked up to the counter to get my pretzel. I looked forward to getting one every time we visited the city. As I stood in line, there was a tall, African-American male in front of me. I remember him being close to 6 foot 6 inches tall and wearing a trench coat. The guy behind the counter looked at him and asked him what he wanted. "Could I please have a piece of chicken?" The worker pulled out one piece of chicken, put it on the plate and said, "That'll be $3.00."

The tall man responded, "I'm sorry, but I don't have the money. Since it is Christmas, would you be kind enough to give me a piece of chicken? I haven't eaten today." The guy behind the counter looked at him with a grim face and screamed, "Get outta here, you bum!" The tall man in the trench coat looked down at me. I looked at him. Then I looked at my $3.00. "I'll have a pretzel and a Coke, please." That's what I said. "I'll have a pretzel and a Coke."

I never forgot about that man and say a prayer for him every Thanksgiving and Christmas. I don't know if he's alive or dead. My belief is that hungry man standing in front of me that day was no other than God. He didn't want me to feed him so that I could live a life helping other people going through life hungry. That was the start of my quest to find some way to help those less fortunate than myself. Since that day, I have volunteered numerous hours of my time and much money, to feed those who are going hungry not only in my own city and state, but throughout the United States.

In 2007, I decided to take it to another level. Sure, my display was nice to look at but how could I use it to help those who are hungry? I approached the Connecticut Food Bank and asked if I could host a food drive during the Christmas season using our Christmas display and website. In November, after setting our goal to raise $2,000, I approached the media. I contacted the newspapers (both local and statewide), radio stations and television stations. I did on air interviews and slowly gained notoriety. By the end of December, my wife and I had raised $2,600 for the

Connecticut Food Bank. We exceeded our goal in less than a month. What a wonderful feeling!

Once you find a cause you believe in, you'd be amazed at how easy it is to organize the fundraiser. Contact the charity that you want to help and let them know you're interested in doing a fundraiser for them. Most charities will be happy to accept your invitation and may even help you with some of the planning details. One of the details you will need to iron out is what you will be collecting for the charity. Are you going to accept monetary or non-monetary donations? Ask the charity. More likely than not, they will be able to give you some great ideas to make your fundraiser a success.

The last step in your plan is to contact the media. Start with your local papers, statewide papers, radio personalities and finally the television stations in that order. You will get the most response for your fundraiser from a local T.V. news broadcast, especially if they are on a nationwide channel.

Tip: Remember, newspaper reporters are swamped with emails. If you can, contact the editor. Let them know that you are doing something for a charitable cause and you'll get a faster response.

Lastly, have fun. Remember, it's not how much money you raise. It's the lives that you touch that count.

Now that you have my story, go write your own.

Afterthought

Christmas is a wonderful time when everyone seems to treat each other with a little more respect. People smile at each other more often and want to lend a helping hand to those less fortunate. On the other hand, there are people out there for whom Christmas is not a good time. Maybe they've lost a loved one or they have personal problems and they're feeling depressed. I've had many people thank me for brightening up their day by with my display. It's a wonderful feeling to know that I am able to put a smile on a person who would have otherwise passed by my house sad and depressed. People ask me all the time why I spend months preparing and over two months putting up lights. The answer is to see the happy faces of people walking or driving by looking in amazement at the bright lights. People even stop when I'm putting up the lights in October and thank me for continuing to put a sparkle in their lives. What a great feeling it is to know that I can touch other lives through my display as you will through yours.

It's been a great journey as I've had a lot of fun sharing what I know about decorating a home for Christmas. I hope you had just as much fun learning about the great hobby of Christmas decorating. I also hope that you got some great ideas about how to build your own display.

Remember, you don't have to start big. I didn't. My 1,500 lights have now well surpassed 30,000 lights. Make your display your own. Give it a personality. Let it be reflective of who you are. Your lawn and your home is your canvas. Paint it with lights and make it your masterpiece.

And above all, have fun.

Merry Christmas and best of luck on your display!

Chris

Christmas Links Mentioned

www.thathouseinmilford.com (our display)

www.christmasdepot.com (here's where you can find siding clips)

www.wind-o-light.com

www.planetchristmas.com (a great network for those who love decorating for Christmas)

www.freewebs.com

www.p3international.com (Kill-O-Watt)

www.woodcraftplans.com

www.thewinfieldcollection.com

www.holidaysoft.com

www.lightkeeperpro.com

www.q-see.com

978-0-595-52106-7
0-595-52106-1

Made in the USA
Lexington, KY
10 March 2014